Richard Garnett

Poems from the German

Richard Garnett

Poems from the German

ISBN/EAN: 9783744771467

Printed in Europe, USA, Canada, Australia, Japan

Cover: Foto ©Thomas Meinert / pixelio.de

More available books at **www.hansebooks.com**

By the same Author, fcap. 8vo., 5s.

IO IN EGYPT AND OTHER POEMS.

NOTICES OF THE PRESS.

" Throughout his volume we have ample tokens of a delicate ear and a refined taste. The poems are wonderfully free from the blemishes too often found in the works of modern bards. Either from a natural gift, or by much careful practice, they have about them a finished ease not unlike the shorter pieces of Coleridge. Less condensed than those of Tennyson, they show much of the laureate's subtle fancy and artistic reticence. Their author has the rare merit of knowing when to have done, and what to leave out."—*Dublin University Magazine.*

" The author of ' Io in Egypt' is a young man who has only to do his own powers justice in order to make himself a name among modern poets. It is not often that a first volume contains so much, not only of promise, but of performance, as that before us."—*North British Review.*

" Mr. Garnett's style is pointed and sharp, expressing much in little, with vivid clearness. His own genius may make his own fame, for his lyrics have many lasting characteristics."
Tait's Magazine.

" A volume full of quaint, luxurious, coloured fancy."
Athenæum.

" Mr. Garnett has, by his latest poems, established a clear title to the name of poet. What strikes us next to his perfect description is his perfect finish."—*Critic.*

" Mr. Garnett writes with classic elevation and propriety, and his volume will secure him respect, and with a superior class of readers."—*Leader.*

LONDON: BELL AND DALDY, 186, FLEET STREET.

POEMS FROM THE GERMAN.

BY RICHARD GARNETT,

AUTHOR OF " IO IN EGYPT," ETC.

" Miraturque novas frondes et non sua poma."

LONDON:
BELL AND DALDY, 186, FLEET STREET
1862.

CONTENTS.

		Page
To the Moon	*Goethe*	1
Mignon's Song	,,	4
Clärchen's Song	,,	6
Serenade	,,	7
The Song of the Archangels	,,	9
Sunset	,,	11
The Shepherd's Lament	,,	14
Huntsman's Song	,,	16
In Absence	,,	18
In a Glade	,,	19
Bokhara no reserve I make	,,	21
The God of Youth	*Hölderlin*	22
A Vision	*Uhland*	26
The Boy of the Mountain	,,	29
O youth, when thou pursuest	,,	31
Resolution	,,	32
The Roe	,,	34
The ancient heroes came to me	*Rückert*	35
Amphion's Lyre	,,	37
The Garden's Denizen	,,	39
To my Infant Daughter	,,	41
Quatrains	,,	44
Phantasy, Wit, and Reason	,,	47
Oft, when Love hath lighted	,,	49
When the shades are turning	,,	50
Zobir	*Platen*	51

Contents.

		Page
Reverie	*Platen*	56
In the Night	,,	59
To ——	,,	61
Ye birds on limber boughs that swing .	,,	62
Spring did a nuptial feast proclaim . .	,,	63
The House of Childhood	*Brentano*	64
The Fisher	,,	69
Serenade	,,	75
Valkyrs	*Heine*	76
Three and Two	,,	78
The Tempest	,,	82
The Asra	,,	84
Ottilia	,,	86
Agnes	,,	88
Songs	,,	90
The Three	*Lenau*	95
In Moonlight	,,	97
Roses, roses gathering	,,	100
Ammonium	*Freiligrath*	102
To my Pompeian Lamp	*Lingg*	104
Autumnal	,,	107
Back to my home I turn'd, and found it .	,,	108
Light my sleep and lighter ever . .	,,	110
A serious man am I, whose every word .	*Schefer*	111
Every point of Love is fair . . .	,,	112
What boots it that the violet shy . .	,,	113
Adam's Sacrifice	*Hebbel*	114
An Emblem	,,	115
In garb of gold and purple . . .	*Deutsch*	116
I thought upon my country . . .	,,	118

POEMS FROM THE GERMAN.

TO THE MOON.

AS thou fillest glade and lea
   With thy misty shine,
All my soul is drawn to thee,
   Taken into thine.

All my field, beneath thy ray,
   Soften'd I descry;
Like my own grief look'd away
   By a friendly eye.

Every ancient thrill again
    Doth my heart possess,
Wanders on 'twixt joy and pain
    In the loneliness.

Flow, flow on, dear brook; but gay
    Never shall I be;
So delight has flow'd away,
    And fidelity.

Once, alas! was wholly mine
    Earth's most precious gain;
Far too precious to resign,
    And, ah! to retain.

Ripple, brook, in silver break
    Forth the vale along;
Ripple on, and rippling make
    Music to my song;

To the Moon.

When thou, in the wintry eve,
    Dost thy banks o'erflow,
Or the virgin buds receive
    Yet a greener glow.

Blest who, hating not, but yet
    Shunning earthly noise,
Wanders with a friend from it,
    And with him enjoys

Feelings which, to men unknown,
    Or forgotten quite,
Roam the silent breast alone
    In the silent night.

MIGNON'S SONG.

KNOW'ST thou the land where flowers the citron-bloom,
And golden orange glows in leafy gloom?
A soft wind flutters from the fair blue sky,
Still stands the myrtle and the laurel high:
Know'st thou the land?
                      O there, O there,
My Friend, my Love, might thou and I repair!

Know'st thou the house? on pillars rests its roof,
The high hall shines, the chamber gleams aloof,
And marble statues stand and gaze on me,—
What is it they have done, poor child, to thee?
Know'st thou the house?
                      O there, O there,
My Friend, my Guide, might thou and I repair!

Know'st thou the mountain-path, in vapours grey
Immersed? the slow mule picks his foggy way;
In caves abide the dragon's ancient brood;
Crashes the rock, and over it the flood.
Know'st thou the path?
                      O there, O there,
My Friend, my Father, let us both repair!

CLÄRCHEN'S SONG.

Cheerful,
    And tearful,
And thoughtful to be;
Waiting,
Debating,
Irresolutely;
Cast into darkness,
Shouting above,
O! happy alone
Is the heart with its love.

SERENADE.

O, NOT thine eye unsealing,
    Give half a dreaming ear
While sweet my strings are pealing :—
    Sleep, what would'st more, my dear?

While sweet my strings are pealing,
    The stars bless, beaming clear,
The deep eternal feeling :—
    Sleep, what would'st more, my dear?

The deep eternal feeling
    Doth lift me from the sphere
Of earthly rout and reeling :—
    Sleep, what would'st more, my dear?

All earthly rout and reeling
    Thou mak'st to disappear,
'Mid gloom and still concealing :—
    Sleep, what would'st more, my dear?

'Mid gloom and still concealing,
    Giv'st half a dreaming ear,
While sweet my strings are pealing :—
    Sleep, what would'st more, my dear?

THE SONG OF THE ARCHANGELS.

NOW, as hath ever been, the sun
   Makes music 'mid his brother-spheres,
As his predestined course to run
   With steps of thunder he careers;
New strength the gazing angels draw,
   Though he be comprehended never;
Thy works, O Lord, Creation saw
   Sublime, sublime are they for ever!

And swifter far than tongue can say,
   The circling Earth in splendour ranges,
And the fair glow of Eden-day
   With deep and awful night exchanges;
The waters foam up from the ocean,
   And scourge the rocks with frenzied force,

And the swift spheres' eternal motion
    Whirls all along in breathless course.

And fury of unbridled storms
    On every land and sea has birth,
And raging in contention forms
    A chain of terror for the earth;
The thunder crashes—on its way
    The lightning flames forth to destroy,
But the mild process of Thy day
    Thy servants, Lord, revere with joy.

And we are strengthen'd to all time
    By scanning what we fathom never;
The first day saw Thy works sublime,
    And they are still sublime for ever!

SUNSET.

(FAUST *loquitur*.)

O HAPPY he
   Who yet may hope to rise from error's sea!
Our little lore is little aid, and what
   Perchance were worth the knowing, we know not.
Yet be not the last ray of this fair day
   Dimm'd by the plaints of an uneasy mind;
Lo! where the sun sinks bright, and bathes in light
   The huts with countless clustering leaves entwined!
It sinks, the orb has lived his term of life,
   Yet westward wending, he recruits his ray,
O for a wing to lift me from this strife,
   Plant me in heaven, and launch me on his way!

Girt with the rich resplendence would I sail,
    And watch the wide world at my feet unroll'd,
Each hill alit, a calm on every vale,
    And every brook a wandering thread of gold.
Not all the savage mountains' soaring peaks
    Were barriers to impede my godlike flight,
The spreading sea to her remotest creeks
    Lay as a map 'neath my undazzled sight.
The sun at length in night's cold clasp must fade,
    But what avails my ardent course to bind?
I chase the fleeting splendour undismay'd,
    The day before me and the night behind,
The unbounded heaven above, the unbounded sea
    Below.—Bright vision, art thou vanishing?
Forbear thy dreams, fond soul, 'tis not for thee
    To beat immortal air with mortal wing.
Yet is there not a son of clay, but feels
    Some high emotion in his breast take birth,
When, from the blue that her frail form conceals,
    The lark's glad song descends to earth,

When eagles wide their wings expand
  O'er the steep mountain's piny crest,
And o'er long wastes of sea and land
  The crane steers to her southern nest.

THE SHEPHERD'S LAMENT.

HERE, here upon the mountain
    A thousand times I stand,
And on my staff I lean me,
    And look upon the land.

My feeding flocks I follow,
    My good dog keeps them well,
And now I have descended,
    And how I cannot tell.

And here with vivid flowerets
    The mead is all aglow;
I stoop me and I pluck them,
    For whom I do not know.

The Shepherd's Lament.

Beneath the tree I house me
   In tempests' roar and gleam;
Her door is shut against me,—
   Alas, 'twas all a dream!

A rainbow, like a vision,
   Stands o'er that simple home;
But she, she hath departed,
   And far away doth roam;

Far over the land, and haply
   Far over the bitter sea;—
Move on, my sheep, move onward,
   And, shepherd, woe is thee!

HUNTSMAN'S SONG.

WITH ready gun, with heavy heart,
    O'er hill and dale I rove,
And ever in my sight thou art,
    Sweet vision of my love!

Thou stealest on by glade and heath,
    A lovely, silent thing;
O, can my image o'er thy path
    Be likewise hovering?

Who leaves thee, slow must be his pace,
    And sore his heart oppress'd,
If to the East he set his face,
    Or if unto the West.

Yet, when I muse upon thee, lo!
   A deep, a blissful boon
Comes purely o'er my breast, as though
   I look'd unto the moon.

IN ABSENCE.

AND wilt thou then no more be mine?
    How can it be thou art not here,
When every word and tone of thine
    Rings plain in the familiar ear?

As when the traveller doth raise
    His sight, and fruitlessly pursue
The singing lark, lost to his gaze
    In sunlight and unbounded blue,

So all around and everywhere
    My restless sight is strain'd for thee,
And all my songs one burden bear,—
    O come, Beloved, back to me!

IN A GLADE.

IN a glade
   I idly went,
Nought to seek
   Was my intent.

I saw a flower
   In shelter shy,
Fair as a star,
   Sweet as an eye.

I stoop'd to pluck it,
   Then did it say,
" Why be gather'd
   To fade away?"

I gently loosed
    The earth around,
Bore it home to my
    Garden-ground;

In a nook
    The flower I set;
There it grows and
    Blossoms yet.

BOKHARA no reserve I make,
    Or Balkh or Samarcand;
Where is the town I would not take
    And give into thine hand?

But ask the Sultan, whose they are,
    If he such gifts approves?
More great is he and wise by far,
    But knows not how one loves.

O monarch, wouldst thou seek to vie
    In lavishness with me?
Thou must have such a queen as I,
    And such a beggar be.

THE GOD OF YOUTH.

WHEN, in the silent even,
   Or 'neath the summer night,
Thy spirit searches Heaven
   For visionary light;
If in the silent spaces
   Thou deemest yet to see
The pale majestic faces
   Of high antiquity;

If a God's incarnation,
   In Beauty's guise array'd,
Thy spirit's aspiration
   Can momently persuade
To stoop and linger, bodeful
   Of happiness to be,

And even on its road full
   Of final melody;

Then seek the stillest valley's
   Most flowery recess,
And pour from golden chalice
   The wine of happiness,
Thy bosom's spring, unwaning,
   Is smiling yet on thee,
The God of Youth is reigning
   Yet over thee and me.

As in the walks of Tibur,
   When, rapt in dreams sublime,
The poet of the Roman
   Forgot the flight of Time;
Soothed by the elm-tree's whisper,
   And freedom of thy flow,
Thou blossom-lipping lisper,
   O crystal Anio!

As by the halls of Plato,
   When, ringing through the grove,
The nightingale saluted
   The shining star of Love;
When all the winds were breathless,
   And, bearer of the swan,
Cephisus through the olive
   And myrtle-thickets ran:

So fair is Earth yet, matting
   The meadow with her flowers,
As erst in the grave Latin
   And sweet Athenian hours;
As grand the sky nocturnal,
   As pure the sky of day,
The bosom as fraternal
   With melody and May.

Then seek the stillest valley's
   Most flowery recess,

And pour from golden chalice
   The wine of happiness;
The joy of earth, unwaning,
   Is smiling yet on thee,
The God of Youth is reigning
   Yet over thee and me.

A VISION.

EVEN now I had a vision;
    I lay upon a steep;
It was by the sea-strand,
I look'd upon the land,
    And out unto the deep;

And by the sea-shore ready,
    A gallant vessel lay,
With colour'd flags all blowing,
The pilot coming, going,
    Impatient of delay.

Then from the distant mountains
    Came down a gallant train,

Like angels bright, bedeck'd
With flowers, and direct
    They moved unto the main.

Before that gay procession
    Fair children did advance;
The rest made music, sung,
The empty goblet swung,
    And interwove the dance.

They said unto the pilot,
    " Come, wilt thou take us forth?
The Loves and Joys are we,
And now would put to sea,
    And all forsake the earth."

Then all those dear companions
    Into his boat he bade,
Inquiring, " Say, ye kind,
Are any left behind
    On mountain, or in glade?"

"None," said they; "speed us quickly,
　We may not tarry here."
Swiftly the sea they cleft;
I saw the earth bereft
　Of all that made her dear.

THE BOY OF THE MOUNTAIN.

THE mountain shepherd-boy am I,
  Beneath me all the valleys lie,
Here on my dwelling-place is cast
The earliest sunlight, and the last,—
  I am the boy of the mountain !

Here hath the stream its rocky birth,
I drink it ere it leaps to earth ;
Its waters none but I restrain,
I breast them, hurl them back again,—
  I am the boy of the mountain !

The mountain-peak is all my own,
Around me all the storms are blown ;

And let them howl from south to north,
Still shall my pealing voice go forth,—
   I am the boy of the mountain!

The thunder and the lightning too
Pass under me, so high in blue,
I know the thunderbolts, and call,
" Hurt not my father's house at all;"—
   I am the boy of the mountain!

And when the tocsin rings, and leaps
Fire after fire on all the steeps,
I hurry down my mates among,
And swing my sword, and sing my song,—
   I am the boy of the mountain!

O YOUTH, when thou pursuest
    What never can be thine,
And passionately wooest
    The reachless and divine,
The prayer kind Heaven hearkens
    It smilingly denies,
And soon no sorrow darkens
    Thy bosom or thine eyes.

But when from every folly
    The heart has turn'd away,
And seeks the noble wholly,
    The good and perfect way,
And still it is forbidden,
    And backward still is thrown,
O be its tears unchidden,
    And give it of thine own!

RESOLUTION.

SHE'LL come along this pathway wild,
    To-day I go adventuring;
Why should I quake before the child
    That never harm'd a mortal thing?

They hail her all, so glad they are:
    I pass along and dare no glance,
Nor ever to the fairest star
    Uplift my foolish countenance.

The flowers that greet her going by,
    The birds with reckless songs of glee,
Love unforbidden testify,
    Then wherefore my timidity?

Night after night have I declared
    My trouble to the Powers above;
But she from me has never heard
    The monosyllable of love.

Here will I lie beneath the tree
    Her punctual footsteps never miss,
And, feigning a soliloquy,
    Will say how very dear she is.

Here will I—O the consternation!
    She's coming on, she's drawing nigh!
Here in this bush I'll take my station,
    And watch her as she passes by.

THE ROE.

A HUNTSMAN hunted many an hour
    A roe by field and flood,
Till saw he where, 'mid tree and flower,
    A charming maiden stood.

What hath befallen the good horse?
    Can he have cast a shoe?
What hindereth the huntsman's course,
    And checks his clear halloo?

By mountain and by valley-path
    Yet panting runs the roe;
Stop, foolish thing, the huntsman hath
    Forgot thee long ago.

THE ancient heroes came to me,
    Requiring I should sing their fame;
I said: " Here is no place for ye,
    One hath me utterly, the same,
Heroic since the world begun,
    Whose shades and signs alone ye were,
Whose bannerals are moon and sun,
    And his encampment sky and air;
Ye fought for petty spans of ground
    In petty spans of time; but he
Monarch eternally is crown'd,
    And his domain infinity.
More ardent fleets this blood, more worth
    Streams in this breast's ennobled veins
Than e'er from gaping wounds gush'd forth
    For wither'd wreaths on brazen plains.

What can a mortal hand essay
    Worthy a mortal heart to move?
The serious deed is childish play,
    And great the littleness of Love.
Here sleeps he in triumphant rest,
    The worlds swing dreamily along,
His cradle-throne my loved one's breast,
    His victor-lullaby my song.

AMPHION'S LYRE.

BY hill and valley treading,
  And singing with the streams,
I saw the world lie red in
  The early morning beams.
With what another vision
  That scene did I descry
Since Love, with glow Elysian,
  Had purged my inner eye!
O happy earth, for ever
  Adorn'd where'er I roam,
On mountain or by river
  Where is the sweetest home?
I said, and sat beholding
  The landscape growing wide,

In every nook unfolding,
    And bright on every side;
When, from the rosy portal
    Before the morning-fire,
The hand of an Immortal
    Reach'd down to me a lyre.
" I am," it whisper'd, golden
    With accents musical,
" Wherewith Amphion olden
    Did build the Theban wall.
If to thy feebler touches
    No thronging homes be shown,
Thou marvel not, but much 'tis
    If thou canst build thine own!
Behold the green profusest
    All swathed in golden air;
Where is the mead thou choosest
    To dwell with me and her?"

THE GARDEN'S DENIZEN.

THE garden's denizen
   Am I, awaiting when
It liketh thee that thou
Should'st visit me, and how.

If as a sunbeam bright
Thou comest, to thy light
This breast shall ope, and be
What hue it pleaseth thee.

Or whether thou be fain
To seek me in the rain,
Or dew, behold Love's cup
To gather thee all up.

Or if it be thy mind
To fan me in the wind,
My bending shall express
My happy thankfulness.

The garden's denizen
Am I, awaiting when
It liketh thee that thou
Should'st visit me, and how.

TO MY INFANT DAUGHTER.

MAY a father without blame
    Of his child enamour'd be?
That am I! now candle-flame
    Melts away the gloom from thee,
Dear little daughter mine, still-nestled on my knee.

    From the study, lone and chill,
    To the nurs'ry's warmer air
    Fled I, while my boys were still
    Sporting out in the free air;
I took her to my heart, and long I held her there.

    As we two, with measured pace,
    Up and down the room did go,

To mine own I press'd her face,
Patiently she left it so,
Something was meant thereby, she fully seem'd to know.

And the while that thoughtfully
Strode I, and she mutely clung,
Strains of old came back to me,
Long unwonted to my tongue—
The songs of love that I erst to her mother sung.

Where these fingers traced them plain
Rest they, by this eye unread,
'Tis not mine to wreathe again
Flowers already garlanded,
And deeper, sweeter themes possess the mother's head.

" Therefore," this with speechless speech
Breathed I as I walk'd, but she

All my meaning seem'd to reach,
Smiling apprehensively,
" Thy parents' hoard of song be dedicate to thee!

" Nought will thy dear mother heed,
Pleased with all that pleaseth me,
Meet for her is meet indeed
For herself renew'd in thee,
So take what for a space must seem a mystery.

" Sure I am, if faith be due
To high mood and pure intent,
Nought is written there, untrue,
From the inmost heart unsent,
Or that a maid may read and not be innocent.

" When thou with thy bridegroom fain
Walkest blithe and soberly,
May he sing thee sweeter strain
Than thy mother heard from me,
Not envied by thy sire for that more than for thee!"

QUATRAINS.

WHO is in love, and evermore
    To all the world doth show it,
Decidedly he is a bore,
Or else he is a poet.

Who Love's commingled cup would drain,
And sweet without the sour obtain,
Would to the shrine at Mecca roam,
And yet be all the while at home.

If thou would'st in the wall be shown,
And have us look unto thee,
Then certainly thou must, O stone,
Consent to let us hew thee.

If somewhat, thou ambitious thing,
Thou would'st be, and not every thing,
Whence this astonishment to view
That other folks are somewhat too?

New to thee,
Meet for thee;
Chaff to me,
Wheat for thee.

Fly, if ye will, this world so mercenary,
But don't be, then, for its applause solicitors;
'Tis odd, to set up for a solitary,
And then complain because one has no visitors.

Care is the common burden, set
On all our backs, my brothers;
The part that each one hath of it
Is ease to all the others.

THE sun would weep himself quite damp
To see on earth so many a scamp,
Would break into pieces and fall into bits—
If it were not for the hypocrites.

THOU shalt not make a lamentation
For all thy earthly hopes' frustration
Till thou canst swear, and take it on thee,
That all thou fear'dst has come upon thee.

To love the best of all
Not oft doth it befall to thee;
Rather to what thou lov'st doth it befall
To seem the best of all to thee.

PHANTASY, WIT, AND REASON.

On a hill sat Phant'sy, covering
    Quite the half;
By her that abbreviated thing,
Wit, the dwarf.
Not at all
Too short or tall,
But a betweenity, like me or you,
Stood Reason, watching the eccentric two.

Phantasy, half to high heaven upraised,
Caught a star,
Shook it, flung it, that the sparks outblazed
Near and far.
Quick as light
The little mite

Darted and dived and overtook the rocket,
Button'd up the sparks into his pocket.

Phantasy a cloud down from the sky
Reach'd, swathed all
Round her shoulders, purple in its dye,
Like a pall.
Sits therein
The mannikin;
Let but a plait be stirr'd, the moment after
The elfin face peeps forth with grinning laughter.

Phant'sy oped her mouth with thunder-word,
Wit bedumbing;
The giantess is still, the dwarf is heard
Whistling, humming.
Reason loses
Patience, chooses
Rather to go,—" Won't do at all for me,
This looks remarkably like Poetry!"

OFT, when Love hath lighted
   All within my breast,
Hath he unrequited
   Been, and I unblest.
Yet, have hearts of others
   Turned to me, unseen,
Trust me, then, my brothers,
   Sadder have I been.
Love to miss, so rarely
   Present from the first!
Wretched Fate, then, fairly,
   Thou hast done thy worst.

WHEN the shades are turning
  Lakewards from the hill,
Feels the heart a yearning,
  Pining to be still;
When the gulls are breasting
  Air towards the sea,
Then would I be resting,
  Heart's delight, with thee.
'Neath the morning heaven
  Gaily do we roam,
Ever in the even
  Would we be at home.

ZOBIR.

IT is a fanatic and pillaging horde
   Of Saracen lances, Abdallah their lord,
And now before thee
Their leaguer is gather'd, O fair Tripoli.

But ere they have struggled and storm'd through
      the breach,
Lo! Gregory's host, and a hero is each,
Byzantium sends
Him, dread of the foeman and stay of his friends.

And as he represses the Saracens' pride,
His golden-hair'd daughter rides on at his side;
A suit hath she donn'd
Of armour, and sports with the spear as a wand.

She hath arm'd her her faith and her land to protect,
The sword doth she brandish, the arrow direct;
And, fair as the sun,
A Pallas doth seem and a Venus in one.

Her father arose, and, surveying his band,
With mighty allurement made stronger each hand;—
" Short work, my brave hearts!
Press onward, and aim at Abdallah your darts.

" Who brings me the head of the chieftain, that day
Maria's white hand shall his valour repay,
A matchless reward!
And treasure uncounted shall own him for lord."

Then doubled the Christians' might; in the brunt
The crescent grew pale, and the scimetar blunt;
Abdallah is fain
To ride to his tent with a slackening rein.

But in that dark camp was a dauntless Emir,
A levin of battle, they call'd him Zobir,
In irefullest mood,
His rattling spurs all bedripping with blood,

He sped to his leader, and cried, " Thou essayest,
Abdallah, the battle no more! and delayest,
With jav'lin unhurl'd,
Who wert for the Caliph to conquer the world.

" Our hosts are discouraged, the Christians' guile
Repay thou in turn with a Saracen wile;
And, promisers both,
Abdallah's be set against Gregory's oath.

" Proclaim it aloud, to thy bands be it said,
' Who severs and brings to me Gregory's head,
Maria shall take,
And lead as a bride for his exploit's sake.' "

As counsels Zobir, so Abdallah has done;
Encouraged, his hosts press victorious on;
The foe fly in fear,
And Gregory falls 'neath the sword of Zobir.

No ramparts the rout of the Christians stem,
The Saracens follow and enter with them;
The banner of green
On Tripoli's every turret is seen.

The Mussulman might long Maria defies;
At length, all surrounded, the enemy's prize,
With many a tear,
She yields to her fate, and is led to Zobir.

And one of the foremost, " To thee do we bring
The meed of thy valour, that marvellous thing
That gave unto thee
Thy glory, our Prophet his fair Tripoli."

The champion heard, and return'd with a smile,—
" The heart of a hero what face can beguile?
What blandishment draw
Aside from the One and his paramount law?

" Fear not, ye bold wooers, no rival am I!
But thee, I release thee, go, maiden, and fly;—
My bride be my spear!
Thou, weep for thy father, and rail at Zobir."

REVERIE.

IN yearning moods I gladly dream
    Myself remote from mortal crowds,
A glider down a silent stream,
    A gazer on the shadowy clouds.

Thrilling and sweet, through all the air,
    Ring summer-birds' care-charming songs;
And waters rock the boat they bear
    Far from the world and all her wrongs.

But seldom to the brink I urge
    My lonely bark, nor leave it then;
But snatch one rosebud from the verge,
    And cleave the watery path again.

Remote, I view the pasturing sheep,
    The flowery change from day to day,
And careful girls their vineyard keep,
    And scythes lay low the new-made hay;

And taste alone the liquid space
    Of light the heavens serenely pour,
And the pure river-drops that chase
    The blood no fleeter than before.

ANSWER.

WHAT would this vague despondency?
    This craving indistinct and dumb?
'Tis difficult the world to flee,
    And easier to overcome.

And even could'st thou fly, thine own
    Impatient heart would quickly press
Thee back again, for love alone
    Of man to man is happiness!

Growth to decrease, decay to bloom,
    Stern laws unalterably bind;
The heart is deeper than the tomb,
    The world less awful than the mind.

Thou seest the awfulness, but fleet
    Time and Occasion bear thee by;
The good and evil hour shall meet
    Together in Tranquillity:

And, as the Moon through heaven doth range,
    Now clouded, spotless now and free,
So like that moon thy life shall change,
    And setting is for her and thee.

IN THE NIGHT.

How started I up in the night, in the night,
    A moody, dissatisfied mortal!
The street left behind me, the watch and his light,
Went through in my flight,
In the night, in the night,
    The Gothic old arch and its portal.

The rillet ran on, coming down from the height,
    I bent o'er the handrail with yearning,
And watch'd the bright ripples, as, clear as the sight,
They fleeted so light
In the night, in the night,
    With never a thought of returning.

In the Night.

Above, in the blue inaccessible height,
   The stars' multitudinous splendour
Burn'd round the clear moon, that with purity bright
Made even their light,
In the night, in the night,
More chaste and more tranquilly tender.

I look'd up aloft to the night, to the night,
   And downward again to the chasm.
O woe! thou hast wasted the day and its light,
And now thou must fight
In the night, in the night,
   With grief and a sorrowful spasm!

TO ——

THE form which in designing
    Nature has all her diligence expended,
Remoulding and refining,
More daintily outlining
    Than purest gold by craftsman ever bended:

O wear thou for its armour
    The sober thought that loose desire represses!
Be deaf unto the charmer,
And shun the subtle harmer,
    Whatever hand approach the golden tresses.

Although thou seem elected
    By Love, most frank, nor yet from melancholy
Remote, be Love rejected,
Thy heart with ice protected,
    Or the wild fire will rise and wrap thee wholly!

YE birds on limber boughs that swing,
　　How frank ye are and fresh of wing!
　With voices meet for morning,
That make me feel a moodier thing,
　And mock me with a warning.

'Tis now an hour I glide and go
Your branchy summer-house below,
　And pass the time but sadly
That doth for ye so brightly flow,
　And bear ye on so gladly.

Who, safe in woods' retirement still,
In emerald mead, by glancing rill,
　Leave man, in town and turret,
To build his own nest as he will,
　And his own woe inherit.

SPRING did a nuptial feast proclaim
    By valley and by hill,
With song and instrument:
I was as malcontent
    As if the snow lay still.

And many a jovial guest he bade;
    I was not of the train.
He knew that I, alas!
Slave to her fancies was,
    And for her fetters fain.

Now am I free, now is my spring,
    Now have I joy and balm
From roses in the hedge,
From rivers and their sedge;
    Yet is my joy more calm.

THE HOUSE OF CHILDHOOD.

AN even-lighted glade in
  There stands a house, holy and high;
Thence many a youth and maiden
  Looks forth with a changeful eye.

They change from weeping to laughter,
  From darkness to light they pass,
Whatever their mood, soon after
  It is not what it was.

'Twas there I saw my darling,
  Lightsome and full of joy
As the blossom the young wind fondles,
  And the rougher winds destroy.

And they, the youths and maidens
    Who dwell in this sweet spot,
Poets and spirits and angels
    Are they, and know it not.

They are like the gods and dress them
    Each day in a different guise;
And O, but my heart is heavy,—
    My darling will change likewise.

O darling mine, where art thou?
    I come where thou should'st be,
And look to thy gleaming window
    To look if thou look'st on me.

I will cherish thee and will keep thee
    Truly as ever I can;—
And there in the garden sits she,
    And is with a wealthy man.

Then mattock and spade I buy me,
    Bind a green apron before,
And like to a gardener make me,
    And knock at the rich man's door.

" O rich man, open thy garden,
    For gladness and not for pay,
Thy flowers will I foster and cherish,
    My silver and gold are they."

" Welcome, gardener, welcome!
    Train up my roses higher,
Twine them and wreathe them and net them,
    Fasten them up with wire.

" Draw the leaves thicker and closer,
    Make me a screen so high
That nothing may fly beyond it,—
    A sweet little bird have I;—

" Sweetly and wildly and clearly
    Down in the dell she sings;
The tall trees stoop to hear her,
    The flower at her feet upsprings."

I see my love that weepeth,
    And secretly looks to me;
The tall trees do not tremble,
    No springing flower I see.

O, why didst thou forsake it,
    That beaming house of light?
The gold of thy head is paleness,
    And dim thy eyeballs' sight.

I wander'd to the beach, love,
    Thy shining star to see,
I saw it fall from heaven,
    And sink into the sea.

I saw it fall from heaven,
   And sink into the wave,
And ever my tears run downward
   To seek for thy star in its grave.

THE FISHER.

IT is a youthful fisher,
   And perish'd is his bliss;
Dead is his love and buried,—
   How shall he credit this?

And till the stars' appearing,
   And till the white moonshine,
He tarries for the maiden,
   To row her on the Rhine.

And with the stars' appearing
   The maiden true appears,
And feeble are her footsteps,
   And white the robe she wears.

Then down the flowing waters
    In silence do they glide,
She shivers and she trembles,
    And shudders at his side.

" O love, the night is dewy,
    The winds thy robe unfold;
O, wrap thee in my mantle,
    And screen thee from the cold."

And to the ancient mountains
    Her snowy arms she spreads,
And hails the moon's effulgence
    And silver on the heads

Of huge and hoary castles,
    And in the boat upstands,
And fain would grasp the moonlight,
    And hold it in her hands.

The Fisher.

"O love, upon my bosom
    In peace and stillness rest,
The stream is deep and rapid,
    And death is in its breast!"

Now past the stately cities
    The rapid stream impels;
And in the towers is pealing
    And chiming of the bells.

Then lowly kneels the maiden,
    Her praying palms she folds,
And all the height of heaven
    With sweetest looks beholds.

"Dear maiden, pray in silence,
    And safer shall we float;
I fear the hasty waters
    And swaying of the boat."

Behold, a pious cloister,
    And nuns the holy strains
Are chanting, and tall tapers
    Illume the tinted panes.

And clearly sings the maiden,
    Responding to the lay;
And tearfully she watches
    The fisher-youth alway.

Then chants the youth, replying
    With tearful eye dismay'd,
And wistfully and dumbly
    Doth look unto the maid.

And redder yet and redder
    The kindling river glows,
And whiter yet and whiter
    The maiden's visage grows.

And now the moon is fading,
    And now the stars are few,
And now the maiden's bright eyes
    Are dimm'd and heavy too.

" Good-morrow, dear my maiden,
    And evening too in one,
Why should'st thou sink in slumber
    At waking of the sun?"

And plain he sees the steeples,
    And plainly he perceives
The thousand-voicèd concert
    And rumour from the leaves,

And thinks to wake the maiden
    To share the morning's grace,
And turns, and bends him o'er her,—
    And empty is her place.

Then in the boat he lays him,
    And sobs until he sleeps;
And on and on goes drifting,
    And driving to the deeps.

Now rise the mighty waters,
    And toss like to a toy
The frail unguided barklet,
    And cannot rouse the boy;

But safe amid the billows
    The stately vessels glide,
And see the youth laid sleeping,—
    The maiden at his side.

SERENADE.

LISTEN, mute in golden luting,
    Silverly the brooks reply;
Sweet saluting, gentle fluting,
    Blending, ending tenderly.

Thrills the finger of the singer,
    Thrillingly his heart replies;
Sweetly through the dark unto thee
    Music looketh with my eyes.

VALKYRS.

STILL they combat on the meads,
   High in air on cloudy steeds
Sweep three Valkyrs, and loud rattle
To their shields their songs of battle :—

" Nations war when kings command,
Each would win the other's land,
Sovran sway is sovran good,
Greatest worth is bravest blood.

" No proud helmet now, huzza !
Mocks the fury of the fray ;
Spilt the fiery blood and glorious,
And the dastard is victorious.

" Laurel-crowns and triumph-arches!
Proudly in the morn he marches
Who a better man o'ercame,
And despoil'd of land and fame.

" Burgomaster! Senator!
Crouch before your conqueror,
Hail with shouts your subjugation,
Open to your desolation!

" Multitudes the walls array,
Cymbals clash and trumpets bray,
Clanging church-bells stun the crowd,
And the rabble shout aloud."

THREE AND TWO.

SHY from a sullen rack of clouds
    Upon a stormy sea
Look'd forth the moon, into the boat
    We stepp'd, and we were Three.

The oars with stroke monotonous
    Plash'd down into the sea,
And wild the foaming waves arose,
    And sprinkled us all three.

And in the boat as pale and chill
    And motionless she stood,
As she a marble image were,
    And not of flesh and blood.

Now hides the moon her face, and shrills
    A north wind cold and bleak,
And high above our heads we hear
    An agonising shriek.

It is the white and ghostly mew,
    And at the evil note,
That sounds like voice of warning, we
    All shudder in the boat.

Have I a fever? Is 't a jest
    Of nightly phantasy?
Mocks me a dream? If so, it is
    A ghastly mockery!

A ghastly mockery! I dream
    That I a Saviour am,
And bear my cross of woe extreme
    As patient as a lamb.

Poor beauty, prithee quake not so,
    'Tis I will set thee free
From sin and shame and want and woe,
    And all thy misery.

Poor beauty, prithee quake not so,
    Though hard the cure may be,
My heart will break, and yet I know
    That death is good for thee.

O mockery and evil dream!
    A madman's ghastly lot!
Dark broods the night, loud howls the sea—
    O God, forsake me not!

Forsake me not, thou clement God,
    Thou Merciful! Shaddai!
It plashes in the water. Woe!
    Jehovah! Adonai!

The sun broke, towards the smiling land
    We steer'd our glad canoe,
And when we stepp'd out on the strand,
    Then were we only Two.

THE TEMPEST.

FIERCE streams the blast—in anguish coils
   The wave beneath it, gleams and boils,
And soars with many a foaming fountain,
A white and living water-mountain.
The bark the waves in mockery fling
Forth from their foamy ravening,
A moment gleams—and instant is
Lost in a yawning black abyss.

In vain my prayer and deprecation;
Drown'd in the shock and agitation
Of the wild winds that raving battle,
And roar, and shriek, and howl, and rattle,
Like one vast cell of maniac sound—
Yet hear I 'mid the broil resound

The gusty accents of a lyre,
And twanging chords, and voice of fire
That tear the shuddering soul along,
And hearkening know whence comes the song.

Far on the rugged Scottish shore,
Where the old castle gazes o'er
The frantic waters in amazement—
There, at the lofty vaulted casement,
A pallid lovely woman stands,
Tender of glance and frail, her hands
Clang on the harp, and wild she sings,
And wild the storm her tresses flings,
And bears the voice of her emotion
Far o'er the roaring wastes of ocean.

THE ASRA.

DAILY walk'd the Sultan's daughter
In the gloaming, by the water,
Where the fountain, rising brightly,
Waver'd o'er the basin lightly.

Daily would the young slave glide
By the stream at eventide,
Where the water plash'd so gaily,—
Pale was he, and paler daily.

Came the Sultan's daughter nigher,
On one eve with words of ire:—
" I thy name will understand,
And thy kindred, and thy land."

" Mohamet the name bestow'd
On me, Yemen my abode,
And the Asra gave me breath,
Whose love ever is their death!"

OTTILIA.

IN treacherous dreams I win my youth again,—
    It is the country-house that crowns the hill;
And down the winding path that seeks the plain
    I joyous wander with Ottilia still.

How blithe her blooming countenance! Her sweet
    Blue eye with merry malice twinkling shines,
And firmly stands she on her little feet,
    And strength with symmetry of frame combines.

The accent of her voice is true and tender,
    Revealing every secret of her mood,
And keenest wit illumed with fancy's splendour
    Darts from the mouth that seems a damask bud.

'Tis not the net of folly that ensnares me,
    I wander not, my reason firmly stands,
The spell of her whole being 'tis that bears me
    With quivering lips to press her snowy hands.

Methinks at length I stoop and pluck a lily,
    And giving it I tremble, and breathe low,—
" Give me thy heart and hand, my sweet Ottilie,
    That I may be as blest and good as thou ! "

Her answer must remain uncomprehended,
    For suddenly I wake, and once more find
Myself a sick man, on my couch extended
    Long years with tortured frame and troubled
        mind.

AGNES.

THOU wert a blonde-hair'd maid without a stain,
So neat, so prim, so cool! I stay'd in vain
To see thy bosom's guarded gates unroll,
And Inspiration breathe upon thy soul

A zeal and ardour for those lofty themes,
By chilly Reason scorn'd for airy dreams;
But wringing from the noble and the good
The toil of hand, and heart, and brain, and blood.

On hills with vineyards' clambering leafage gay,
Glass'd in the Rhine, we roam'd one summer's day,
Bright was the sun, and from the shining cup
Of every flower a giddy scent flew up.

A kiss of fire, a deep voluptuous blush,
Burn'd on each pink and every rosy bush,
Ideal flames in dandelions glow'd,
And lit each sorriest weed that edged our road.

But thou went'st on with even-stepping feet,
Clad in white satin, elegant and neat;
No child of Netscher's brush more trim and nice,
And in thy stays a little heart of ice.

SONGS.

I.

IT was a mighty monarch's child,
  Her cheek was pale, her eyes were wild;
Beneath a linden's shade I press'd
The maiden to my panting breast.

" I will not have thy father's throne,
I will not have his golden crown,
I will not have his realm so wide,
I will have thee, and nought beside."

" That cannot be," the maiden said,
" Because I am already dead,
And but by night the sods above
I burst for thee and thy dear love."

II.

The rose and the lily, the moon and the dove,
Once loved I them all with a perfect love;
I love them no longer, I love alone
The Lovely, the Graceful, the Pure, the One,
Who twines in one wreath all their beauty and love,
And rose is and lily and moon and dove.

III.

Who was it, tell me, that first of men reckon'd
Time by the hour and the minute and second?
A soulless man, without heat or light;
He sat and he mused in the long winter's night,
And counted the pittering steps of the mouse,
And the pick of the woodworm that gnaw'd at the house.

Kisses, now tell me, who first did discover?
It was the warm happy mouth of a lover.

He kiss'd without ceasing, he kiss'd without care,
He kiss'd his first kiss in the May-season fair;
The flowers from their emerald cradle upsprung,
The sun brightly beam'd, the birds sweetly sung.

IV.

Upon my darling's beaming eyes
    I plied my rhyming trade;
Upon my darling's cherry lips
    An epigram I made;
My darling has a blooming cheek,
    I penn'd a song upon it;
And if she had but had a heart,
    Her heart had had a sonnet.

V.

O dearest, canst thou tell me why
    The rose should be so pale?
And why the azure violet
    Should wither in the vale?

And why the lark should in the cloud
   So sorrowfully sing?
And why from loveliest balsam-buds
   A scent of death should spring?

And why the sun upon the mead
   So chillingly should frown?
And why the earth should, like a grave,
   Be mouldering and brown?

And why it is that I myself
   So languishing should be?
And why it is, my heart of hearts,
   That thou forsakest me?

VI.

SEE yonder, where a gem of night
Falls helpless from its heavenly height!
It is the brilliant star of Love
That thus forsakes the realms above.

And one by one the wind bereaves
The apple-tree of silvery leaves.
The breezes, in their reckless play,
Spurn them with dancing feet away.

And round and round swims on the pool
The tuneful swan so beautiful,
And ever singing sweet and slow
He sinks into his grave below.

It is so dreary and so dread!
The leaf is wholly witherèd.
The fallen star has flamed away,
The swan has sung his dying lay.

THE THREE.

THREE warriors that softly ride
From a lost field at eventide;

From their deep wounds the warm streams break,
Courser and saddle glow and reek.

Slow move the steeds, weary and spent,
Else were the gush too violent;

And close they ride, and closely each
Holds by his fellow in his reach,

And sadly look they on the death
In either's visage, and one saith:—

The Three.

"Woe for the maiden and the home
Where these cold feet shall never come!"

"Woe for my meadow-lands and trees,
Castles and vassal villages!"

"The light of heaven is all I have;
There are no windows in the grave."

Three vultures, dissonant and black,
Fly gloating on the bloody track;

Shrieking among themselves they cry,—
"Thou eatest him, him thou, him I."

IN MOONLIGHT.

I THINK of thee, and wander lone
   This spreading river nigh;
O that we listen'd to its tone
   Together, thou and I!

O might we but together glance
   And scan the happy rays
And meekness of the countenance
   The virgin moon displays!

Buoy'd safely on that bridge-like beam
   My eager glances rove,
And range the silver-shining stream
   Up to the darker grove.

And, where a wave of light is cast
    The water-waves upon,
I see how fleet these hurry past
    And chase each other on;

But where, outside that brilliant path,
    The stream flows in the dark,
The sound is all my guide, nor hath
    The eye what it may mark.

O maiden, that the hour were bright
    With one regard from thee,
Who art the splendour of the night,
    And silverness to me!

When, heedless of my bosom's strife,
    Thou roamest far apart,
Dead is the dismal stream of life,
    And stagnant in my heart.

In Moonlight.

But when, thy light reminist'ring,
    That stream thou dost survey,
It ripples blithe and glittering,
    And fleetly flows away.

ROSES, roses gathering,
    Roses of the rarest,
How I would that I might bring
    Them to thee, my fairest!

But, ere I had carried them
    Far, to thee retreating,
Every rose had fled the stem,
    For the rose is fleeting.

Further from his Love to stray
    Be not Love persuaded
Than the hand of lover may
    Bear the rose unfaded,

Than the nightingale doth bring
   Straws and sedges nestward,
Or her music, vibrating,
   Wanders from the westward.

AMMONIUM.

"REST, stranger, while thy courser grazes;
O, travel on no more this night!
Stay by the greenest of oases,
That shines amid the sandy places
As when a topaz-wreath enchases
An emerald's pure, refreshing light!"

" Thanks for your hospitable proffer!"
He said, and lighted down from his
Steed on the grass, and sat down over
Against his hosts, while past did hover
The vulture, flying to recover
Her eyrie in Pentapolis.

A sound of song and joyous dances;
Wide on his knees he spread his book:
The tents, the fires, the steeds, the lances,
The swart Arabian countenances,
The beards, the shields—like wild romances,
These things his ardent fancy took.

He sat with busy pencil stealing
An image of his desert rest;
By the clear spring were camels kneeling;
The lissom Arab maids, revealing
Their features half, and half concealing,
Sang, fleeting round their Christian guest:—

" Rest, stranger, while thy courser grazes;
O, travel on no more this night!
Stay by the greenest of oases,
That shines amid the sandy places
As when a topaz-wreath enchases
An emerald's pure, refreshing light!"

TO MY POMPEIAN LAMP.

NO, comforter, we will not sever!
    My trusty lamp, whose modest glow,
When the torn nerves in agony quiver,
Pour'd mildly, saith, " Hope on, not ever
                Shall this be so!"

To thee my oil shall ne'er be scanted,
Could the pale spell the poppy hath
Repay the fellowship enchanted
Of thee to whom 'tis nightly granted
                To light my path

To Helicon? my path who drew thee
From charnels Neapolitan

To the clear day, and did renew thee
With light unused, which now unto me
    Shines all it can!

Rememberest thou thy home? how play'd
The fountain, sent with genial flow
Forth from a marble mask, and made
Music all night in colonnade
    And portico?

Rememberest thou the chamber, say,
And him of quiet mien antique
Who nursed thy flickering light alway,
And seal'd his letter by thy ray,
    And spoke in Greek?

'Mid the pale shades, my gentle mate,
By the pure sun unvisited,
Hast slept this many a year, by weight
Of wrack and ruin desolate,
    Bound to the dead?

To my Pompeian Lamp.

The slumberer's breath, the night-wind's sway,
Once more thou hearkenest, nothing loth,
From tree and flower thy witching ray
Seduces yet again the grey
    And fickle moth.

My soul, that did thy soul restore,
Soon, tiny lamp, must change with thee,
And wander by the Avernian shore,
While thou on high dost lustre pour,
    And tell of me,

Inquiring haply, when her fate
Brings thee dim Psyche in the night,
Art thou his spirit who hath sate
Wrapt in deep converse with me, late
    Feeding my light?

AUTUMNAL.

O'ER shorn fields, grey with misty streaks,
    The late winds pipe and shrilling roam;
Stumbling beneath a load of sticks,
    A widow leads her orphan home.

Here seek they the forgotten grape,
    The harsh sloe there and woolly haw;
In farm and grange the wild doves scrape
    The stray grain dropt in mud and straw;

And here returns on weary feet,
    A poor lorn child of blame and shame,
At last for the last time to greet
    The last of all who own his name.

Back to my home I turn'd, and found it
 The old dear spot by many a sign,
The same the air, the songs around it;
 And yet it was no home of mine.

Sweet sang, in its old channel driven,
 The stream, the deer the old path trod,
A soft string woke old tunes, and Even
 Blush'd on familiar crag and sod;

But at the door where erst, a ranger
 Return'd, I saw my mother wait,
Sat strangely the intruded stranger,
 And O, I felt my heart a weight!

Methought a voice cried, and I started,—
" Fly from this place, nor stay to learn
How whom thou lov'st are all departed,
And never, never will return!"

LIGHT my sleep and lighter ever,
    Like a veil my grief doth quiver,
        Trembling over me.
In dreams I hear thee come and go,
Crying at my shut door below,
I waken then, and the tears flow—
        For thee? Ah no! for me!

Yes, yes, death is this!
Soon another wilt thou kiss
        When I am in my swoon;
Ere yet the March-wind whirls the vane,
Ere yet the thrush begins her strain,
If thou would'st see me yet again,
        Come soon, soon!

A SERIOUS man am I, whose every word
And action seeks the Better evermore.

Long did I muse, and vainly seek to know
If better 'twere, beneath stars' golden gleam
And trembling blossoms, while the nightingale
Debars alone the night from silentness,
To fall asleep, and slumber in thy arms;
Or better, when the sickle of the moon
Reaps silvery paleness from the golden fields
Of the inflaming morn, and overhead
The lark is vocal, in thy arms to wake.

A prudent man will choose the safer part;
I sink in slumber on thy breast at night,
And thou awak'st me early in thy arms.

EVERY point of Love is fair,
Love is perfect everywhere;
Sweet 'tis to see, sweet to be fain,
Sweet to pursue and to obtain;
The memory of Love, how loving!
The loss of Love, how deep and moving!
But, if of all I had the choosing,
My soul were fix'd on the refusing.
Then doth the unreach'd but seem to be
Set at a height more heavenly.
Every point of Love is fair,
Love is perfect everywhere.

WHAT boots it that the violet shy
  So privily doth blow,
When every cloud that roams the sky
  Her mystery doth know?
The south wind seeks the dim retreat,
  And steals her breath away,
And hurries on with hasty feet
  To give it to the day.
But I, my dear delight, will keep
  The treasure I have found,
And not a curious eye shall peep
  On all our fairy-ground;
Nor wrong I thee by this reserve
  And silence of my lays,
What angel is there doth deserve
  To hearken to thy praise?

ADAM'S SACRIFICE.

WITH sweetest fruits, fresh from the bowers,
    To the green mound he hies,
And wreathen leaves, and balmy flowers,
    A fragrant sacrifice.

Blithe is his brow, then, saddening,
    " Alas, my poverty!
The very tribute I would bring
    I borrow, Lord, from Thee."

AN EMBLEM.

A TREE springs in a thirsty land,
    Lone in the barren plain,
Withering beneath the sun's hot brand,
    And stranger to the rain.

From the sere bough, luscious and loose,
    Depends a glowing fruit,
Laden with all the lingering juice
    And life of stem and root.

The rambling breezes soon will shake
    Its mellow richness down,
Ungather'd for another's sake,
    And made not for its own.

IN garb of gold and purple
    The stately day had gone,
And Night, serene and pensive,
    Was softly coming on.

From silent heights of heaven
    Look'd down, on cot and lea,
The moon's pure curve of silver,
    And stars some two or three;

And dews descended, healing
    The faintness of the bowers,
And so the winds were fragrant,
    And like to wingèd flowers;

The quiet birds lay dreamless
    And songless in the nest,
The nightingale was wakeful,
    And warbled for the rest.

'Mid all the magic music,
    And beauty of the glade,
Thou wert my thought, Beloved,
    And thine the song I made.

I THOUGHT upon my country,
   And all my soul was stirr'd,
And in the dreams of darkness
   Meseem'd I was a bird,

That fought against its cage-bars,
   And shook them night and day,
And broke them with its pinions,
   And singing flew away,

And rising, rising ever,
   So loftily did go,
It saw the noisy Ocean
   Move silently below,

And in the dim blue distance
  A strip of green there shone,
That green strip was a country,
  That country was my own.

Nor knew I till this vision
  Had come unto my heart,
Thou dear far land, how very dear
  And very far thou art!

THE END.

www.ingramcontent.com/pod-product-compliance
Lightning Source LLC
Chambersburg PA
CBHW020122170426
43199CB00009B/599